FRACTURED SYMPHONY

FRACTURED SYMPHONY
© Andi Myles / Cathexis Northwest Press

No part of this book may be reproduced without written permission of the publisher or author, except in reviews and articles.

First Printing: 2025

ISBN: 978-1-952869-92-1

Editing & Design by C. M. Tollefson
Cathexis Northwest Press

cathexisnorthwestpress.com

FRACTURED SYMPHONY

Poems
Andi Myles

Cathexis Northwest Press

For all my unwitting collaborators who find themselves in these pages.

Table of Contents

Do Not Forget to Guard the Calmness: An Emergency Action Plan	1
SONATA FRAGILE	**3**
a love story in three parts	5
Recollection	8
Intersection	9
Could we say then, at least, that I am your muse?	10
Abandoned	11
Mimesis	12
Book Sale	13
Same Page	14
The Rescue	15
You asked me to tell you something obvious	16
Relationship Inquest	17
You asked me to tell you something true	18
INTERMEZZO COSMICO	**19**
Fully Known	21
Careless	22
Switch Off the Nebulas on Your Way Out	23
Transfigured	24
HARMONY IN DISCORD	**25**
Domesticated Emotions	27
Ten Dollars	28
Merry-go-round	29
Illumination	30
Marionette, Condition: Fair	31
Rage	32
Fallen	34
Alternate Titles	35
My Neighborhood	36
The Angler	37
Your Birthday	38
Unenlightenment	39

DO NOT FORGET TO GUARD THE CALMNESS: AN EMERGENCY ACTION PLAN

1. SOUND THE ALARM

In a crisis situation, the first thing I notice is how cold my hands are. This is my sympathetic nervous system deciding that I am about to be in some shit. *Sympathetic, it is important to note, not empathetic.* It pulls back the blood from my inept feet that brought me to this place. It claws back the life it has gifted my irresponsible hands and feeds instead my lungs, my heart. The pieces of me that it controls. My body knows

I cannot be trusted. In a crisis situation, it does not matter that I and my body are only sympathetic and that I look with disgust at my form in the mirror. It does not matter that my body despises me for what I feed it—or don't. In a crisis situation, my body and I become one. If my blood is spilled in the melee to come, as my body expects, I will bleed less because of its sympathy.

2. GUARD THE CALMNESS

Visualize your swing, coaches whisper to nine-year-olds, *see yourself hitting the ball.* My mirror neurons detect the delight of my team and craft the laughs that stumble from my lips. They nestle me deeply into the images of stampedes of starving, blood on knives, bullets strewn through homes. At night, I dream of cars sliding slowly on ice towards telephone poles, bonfires under oak trees, and so many stars they wash over me like sea foam. When my body wakes me

in a room that is not mine for a reason I don't yet understand, as I look at the map on my hotel room door, touch the handle to check its warmth, crawl down the hall to the clearly marked emergency exit, and trip down the concrete stairway—I guard the calmness. My body does not know the flames are not real when I dream of fire.

3. FIND A REFUGE

I can tell you when my life began. I was three and believed that I could stop my fall by doing a handstand. My body had no such delusion. It may have lived before then—I had not. When does life end? More important: when does death begin? The first time I forget my child's birthday? Her name? Her? On days when I live

behind my eyes—my entire soul curled like a cat watching a bird outside the window—my abandoned body gushes with adrenaline and I catch it attracting others to itself. It is then that I know, I was not my body's first choice either.

4. FIGHT OR FLEE

This body has been carefully selected over millennia not for happiness, not for perfection, but for survival. In a crisis situation, this body does not know the difference between a surgeon's knife and a lion's claw. It knows only severed skin, disconnected muscles, starved cells, aimless vessels pouring, pouring warm blood onto cool skin. *How will you remember to love me*

when you are dead? my daughter asks. I tell her my atoms will find her atoms and we will become a bird and a tree and a star together. It is the only lie I allow myself to tell her. It calms her and my sympathetic nervous system while I continue down the smokey stairway.

SONATA FRAGILE

a love story in three parts

Chapter I: Stars at Noon

I will not tell you that
you are cold hands on a
warm mug pulling heat from
the depths of me. What I
mean is that you are stars at noon.
That is to say,

unseen, but always there.
You are the moon lit from
behind, in other words,
invisible, hidden,
secret. When you turn your gaze on
me—I forget

my smallness—you eclipse
the sun, my whole world mutes,
darkens. How do I say
this? I want to tell you
that when the oceans reach for you,
my body
feels your pull.

Chapter II: TripTik

The serenity of
maps is a kind of lie.
You, tiny, fit in my
palm, contained—motionless.
No—fixed, immoveable. I plot
my way to you.

Maps demand that we know,
know like mosquitos know
where to prick, like siblings
know your open wounds, sins
unspoken. The problem—to be
sure where you are.

An eclipse requires two
bodies. Behind you, he
obscures the nakedness
of your craters and the
truth—an eclipse needs three bodies,
one to watch as
you eclipse him.

Chapter III: A Warning Against Eclipse Gazing

Look, unencumbered,
at the totality
and you will fall in love
with the moon. You will soon
realize it was never the sun
that you wanted—

the moon, with its softness
its reflection, is what
you crave. They will tell you
the sun gives life, without
it, you wouldn't even see your
moon, you will say,

*Let the plants eat the sun,
I need the darkness.* Keep
the moon at a distance,
in your periphery,
a pleasurable clenching of
your chest when you

see it in the daylight
sky. From someone with an
eclipse burned on my eyes,
let me assure you,
the lighting is always better
in fantasy.

If you look, remember
that you will never see
in the same way again.
It will be worth the pain,
to see my love vanquish the sun.
My dear, we have
all felt this way.

Recollection

You asked me to tell you something real
so I pulled back the sky

to reveal the lights behind the night,
the drywall and pinholed cardboard,

the painted vistas of places
you always meant to see up close

like the alley behind your yard.
Under the sequined sea floor

I showed you the metal box filled
with dreams sent to the aspiring, lifetimes

built from discarded Legos.
Next to the only real tree in the world

I straddled you and ran my tongue
across your skin, breathed memory softly

into the spaces between your fingers,
felt your body remember

regret tastes of burned matchsticks.
Barefoot in the grass I called

to the last of the fireflies—
said, *We were all made for you.*

Intersection

There are things
I know are true,
but I don't believe,
like the moon
affects the tides
or time moves
slower the
faster you run.
There are things
I know are untrue,
but I believe,
like the last of the
light of the eighth
brightest star
began its journey
to us the moment
your craving propelled
me to the floor.
That it was satiation,
propitiation,
an offering to
inverse spirits,
sine and cosine,
meeting once
a lifetime, one
reaching up—
the other down.

Could we say then, at least, that I am your muse?

I built a house of railroad tracks and rubber tires
and painted it turquoise.

Or I changed my name to Deniz
and sold mounds of sunset-colored spices in Istanbul's Grand Bazaar.

Or I brought forth new life from a genome
I created by writing poetry with nucleotides.

Or I sometimes report a problem with a new jet
just so I can take her for another ride.

Or I once dropped a box of canned goods,
and wrote a poem about it.

Or I once dropped a box of canned goods,
and you turned the glittering cans oozing dark juices into a glorious work of art.

My house is my house the way a warm shower
resembles a June rain–
which is to say, not much.
I cannot keep the birds from creating a haven in my roof
or the floorboards from serving as sanctuary for mice and wasps.

It's a hell of a thing, to wake up one day to realize that
in the story of the zombie apocalypse, you would be a zombie—
that your role has only ever been supporting cast.

Abandoned

Sometimes when
we are fighting
I look at your feet
and wonder
*Will I kiss them
when you are dead?*
I think maybe
I will–if only to play
at Mary Magdalene.
People will ask me
about my plans.
What are the plans
of an abandoned shell
washed to shore
filled, for the first time,
with sand
instead of life?

Mimesis

When you come home tonight you will not find me here. If you look carefully (you won't) you will notice an empty paper cup tipped over on the table or a basket of unfolded laundry (perhaps you will wonder, *was that there when I left?*) You will talk to me even though you don't see me because it is unthinkable (to us both) that I could leave. You will address your monologue to the kitchen counter. After all, everyone always says your wife resembles a bowl of grapes.

Book Sale

I left our
book on the A
train—the one
with our love
story in the
margins, our threesome
with an unwitting
Anne Carson—hoping
it would ride
for half an eternity
hauling its earth-
shattering profundity
from Washington
Heights to Jamaica
Bay or be scooped
up by a romantic
college student
and brought south
where you might stumble
across it at a library
book sale only for it
to force to mind
what a petty
unremarkable
love we had.

Same Page

I burned my hand
and you got Shakespeare in the divorce
which feels unfair.

You were beautiful in your knowingness—the
sense that you already knew my secrets, but even more
that I knew yours—

you were a greenish gold shimmering
the good kind of ache, the hero of
our story.

For a few glorious moments,
we read the same pages.
But once you know of Leda, Zeus

never looks the same.
He forever carries with him a bit of swan—
which has always seemed to me a snake.

The Rescue

We are still there, you and I,
pressed against the wall of the lighthouse,
shivering in the ocean spray,
talking loudly about loneliness
as if noise itself could solidify in the space
between us and keep us apart.

We are still there, my eyes are fixed
on your lips, watching, terrified, as the moment
begins to blur with the film of the past,
as it fills itself
       with the surge
              of everything to come.
I am still watching as the fine lines of your face
smear into your older self,
that look of ravenous desire
dwindling into indifference.

I went back there to pull her away from that instant—
the last before we became we. But she watched
as the sheen of the present tarnished into the past
and she chose you.

You asked me to tell you something obvious

    at the end   you become manically vibrant

        or listlessly muted

                I will not be

          asleep at midday   I will drink the sun

buzzing   with plasma joy

how   could I give up

                a moment

      a single kiss

you are   the bird   who nests

        in my soffit   I hate you

     invading   my being

but I love   to watch you fly

        you leaned in   to kiss me

    when   rebuffed you said

      when you die   *you will die*

     with one less kiss   *in your life*

           so I grabbed you   and kissed you and

kissed you

again

Relationship Inquest

    That pastoral landscape
            slightly askew—you plucked

    the last petal; let me go. The ant reaching
            from a frayed grass blade

    to your wicker picnic basket.
    Sneaky   *devil*, you whispered

            before brushing me aside.
    The stem of a ripe strawberry,
            a broken button on your favorite winter coat,
                     a damp, faded dishtowel slouching on the counter.
    I am sorry
            I make you sad.

You asked me to tell you something true

You never touched me—your memory
of sliding your hand slowly down my ribs

to my waist was only the electrons
of my atoms repelled by yours.

How strange, our bodies have forgotten
how to fit together, they have changed

since you nudged me awake under a silvery sky
to repulse my electrons, again and

again, the cathedral aglow in your window.
It is not my touch you miss as we linger

over cold coffee and shredded napkins, it is the time
before you discovered we are always alone.

Don't worry my love, a scalpel can still cut
and as you walk across the ground—you fly.

INTERMEZZO COSMICO

Fully Known

Other universes seep through the cracks
in my walls and for a moment
      my favorite color is no longer blue
        but the orange of my kitchen walls,
        they shiver, suddenly too beautiful
so I do not stay there. When I am
rinsing a chicken for dinner
        I feel the skin slide over the newborn
        bones I chose not to bear, hear it cawing
    in my hands.
I am trying to find the universe
        next to my own where the only difference is
        an extra book on the shelf or
        maybe some soup in the fridge.
Tiptoe down the halls
at night the moaning floors let in
too many possibilities
        sliding my fingertips down her breasts, newspaper clippings
        of success of tragedy of nothing notable, a bruised face,
        small fingers touching my nose, a yapping dog, his lips
        against mine begging, brushing long hair before a mirror—
darkly.
    I am looking
    for a slightly stronger version of
this stranger
I inhabit—it cannot be trusted, it has lived
so many lives.

Careless

The world ended when that snail dried out
on the tacky sunbaked asphalt
and no one noticed that
something continued, but it was not

the world with the snail in it.
I misplaced the world where
this snail is whole
where it was not crushed by the heel of

my elementary school best friend
who told me on the first day of sixth grade
at the outdoor lunch tables
that we could not be friends anymore

because she was in 6B and I was in 6A.
I always wondered, after five years of togetherness,
if our separation was kismet,
or if I was her Eurydice.

While we are looking
for the world that ended,
can you help me find

the first boy whose heart I broke—
his name was Daniel and I
was cruel.

Switch Off the Nebulas on Your Way Out

Andromeda slouches against my front door;
      you'll have to squeeze past her to get in.
           For a galaxy made up mostly of space,

she is remarkably heavy
      but don't tell her I said so.
           The black holes tend to gather around my sinks,

rubbing against each other, joking
      about the strength of their gravity. They love to threaten
           to swallow each other—but they are

all talk. If you fancy a drink, just flatter their egos;
      they'll let you by. Don't bother trying to
         corral the constellations,

they are all hopped up on space dust
      and will scatter if you get too close. Just let them
           roll around under the couch, at least they will keep

the mice away. Stay out of the bedroom—
      the edges of the universe tend to linger there,
           and you don't need to see what lives on the other side.

Transfigured

You will be forever altered
once you stop writing about sex, you know.
Did I say writing? I meant being absorbed by,

like the marriage between
dirty counter water and a dry sponge.
I meant consumed by. Sex likes me best
when I am soaked in gin.

When we are unsteady,
he says, There are ten thousand stars
for every grain of sand, you know,
I don't know, I rarely do.

I swallow the earth with
the sun as a chaser
There are more molecules in a handful
of water than stars in the sky, you know,

mix the remaining planets in a glass
two parts nebula, three parts space dust—
getting drunk on the universe
is the only way to shut him up.

I dream of smoking cigarettes
but I am pregnant with the new earth
bloated with possibility
aching for my final transformation
like a child who loves
the ocean she has never seen.

HARMONY IN DISCORD

Domesticated Emotions

1. Today Frustration came to my door, I told him to join Resentment upstairs.

2. I send Anger away when he calls, but Fatigue—long, lithe, seductive—follows me, curled like a cat at the end of my couch, I rub her fur with my toes.

3. I tell my son to feel what he feels, and he lets Fear in at night to sleep under his bed. But he sets Delight and Affection on his bookshelf where he can keep an eye on them.

4. Lust lives in the attic, he says he likes the cold.

5. Pleasure and Embarrassment go everywhere together, I cannot convince them to unwind.

6. Despair has no fixed place, he sneaks around—sometimes in a drawer, sometimes in the bathtub. Occasionally he hides in the medicine cabinet, waiting to surprise me.

7. Sometimes I call them all down to line up in front of me like the Von Trapp family singers. *Sing*, I command. They harmonize well.

8. Weariness winds himself around the twins Happiness and Sadness, squeezing tightly, suffocating, dimming, diminishing all the rest—except for Disdain, she and Weariness are the best of friends.

9. I use a measuring spoon to scoop lemon tea into my tiny silver tea holder. Excitement hides in the hot water that jumps and sparkles in the air to greet me.

10. Here is a poem:

    If I could brew Ennui,

        I would drink him. If I could measure

            Joy, I would take

    only a teaspoon.

Ten Dollars

When I closed your tender toddler hand
in the car door, the only screams I heard

were my own. You were always stoic in your pain
your frail bird body stretched on my couch,

ribcage rubbing through your skin—when I still
believed I could patch your fractures with sister-love.

You were beautiful, the final stubborn embers
of a dying fire. I see your smirk flash

in my son's eyes and I forget
to remember you are gone—only that siblings

share an equal measure of genes as parents
and children. You were audacious—

wouldn't be surprised if you were offered
a throne to the world you

wished into being—one that is flat
and stark with no capacity for nuance or

for me, who glories in the grays.
You were always the smoldering rage

of daffodils that bloomed before the final frost.
I told you the last time I sent you ten dollars,

I will never forgive myself
if this is the one that finally does you in.

Merry-go-round

I hang on with throbbing fingers
as the same scene flickers over and

over again. Some relent
when the ache overwhelms—not

me. I still have paint chips
stuck in my palms. I won't let go
until the last

what
                if,
what
                    if,
what
                          if

Illumination

Do you love me? I asked my mother,
while she washed dishes.
Do   you   love   me?   I asked

in the evening. I asked like the perpetual
flicker of a fluorescent light.
I asked   not because I doubted,
but because I knew   she did.

I never   asked
my father   because it was obvious
he   did not.
I didn't know   that I knew until

the Chicago winter   swirled
around me as if   I were the
only one   who had braved its embrace.
Streetlamps so close

you'd barely notice the darkness
seeping in.   It is something   to discover
that your father   cannot love.
How absurd   how humiliating to pine

even for love's lackluster simulacrum. Back then
I never walked without music   and Sufjan Stevens
accompanied me   home as I laughed with unleashed
relief to know,   it was never me.

Marionette, Condition: Fair

This body belonged to God
before it belonged to men—

eventually a man, who transformed it
into a fractured vessel belonging

to children. What is this body now,
what use? A puppet with severed strings,

never loved but overused, no value to God—
stained and uncontrollable,

masking tape over a severed middle, nicks and marks
no sanding can smooth—worthless to men.

Knot the strings and paint the knees, but what
do I do with a body that is finally mine?

Rage

I read in the news
that up to a quarter of the
handprints in early cave paintings
came from children
and that, perhaps,
the oldest works of cave art
were a communal activity,
made by toddlers, not
a solitary male pursuit
and of course
because what do you do
with a child in a cave
when it's cold
or when it's hot
or when giant sloths
could come across your toddler
while you are cooking
because of course
the solitary male pursuits
were aligned with survival
because of course survival
was very much not a given
and art only feeds the soul
because of course women
don't make art, or, forgive me,
don't have time to make art
because of course we
still must keep children
from scribbling on the walls
because of-fucking-course
only a solitary male
would ever think otherwise
except
I was surprised
and thought otherwise
and I forgot
that women make art
and children are children
I forgot that of course
art only feeds the soul

and when survival is
very much not a given
choices must be made
when floods fill museums
and masterpieces burn
all that will be left
are smeared chalk drawings
on forgotten streets.

Fallen

A letter to my daughter on the fall of Roe v. Wade

Our mothers lied
telling us the fight was over and failing to mention
the last woman to be burned at the stake has yet to be born.

A job and credit card, too easily satisfied
women dying at man's discretion—
our mothers lied.

Our failure deserves your scorn.
Daughter, lift weights, run fast, live with apprehension
the last woman to be burned at the stake has yet to be born.

Rape—unatoned, power—withheld, we barely tried.
Not the same, not equal, pay attention:
Our mothers lied.

Fearsome bodies—feared—mourn,
mourn. Shaped and sold, recrafted in one dimension,
the last woman to be burned at the stake has yet to be born.

My alarms are tardy and time-worn,
this is your moment of intention:
Our mothers lied
and the last woman to be burned at the stake has yet to be born.

Alternate Titles

The Experience of Having Failed at the Thing Everyone Else Can Do

The Moment No One Else Believes in You Either

The Rush of Almost Being Hit By a Car and the Trembling Limbs from the Adrenaline

The Trembling Limbs That Result from the Orgasm That Took 15 Months to Find

The Power of Making an Irreversible Decision

The Relief of Undoing an Irreversible Decision

The Heartbreak of Knowing You Are Now Too Old to Be the Thing You Always Wanted to Be, Even Though You Always Knew You Never Would

The Pleasure of Waiting to Start the First Page of a New Book by Your Favorite Author Because You Don't Want to Finish It

The Broken Promise to Never Fall in Literary Love with Another Living Author

The Confusion of Never Remembering How to Spell ~~"Maintainence"~~ "Maintenance"

The Mystery of the Potholder That Disappeared from 2016 to 2022

The Job of Getting On with It Despite Wet Socks and No Opportunity to Change Them for Five to Six Hours

The Realization that Your Immune System Could, Should It One Day Be Inspired to, Kill You Faster than Any Infection

The Shock of Seeing an Emotion You Thought You Owned Flash Across the Face of a Toddler

The Beauty of Ambivalence

My Neighborhood

The god of Atlantis sells me fish.
I knew that piece would be perfect for someone,
he says of my choice. I take the paper-wrapped salmon
with all the care the offering deserves.
I know how hard it is when everyone who believes in you
disappears in the same moment.

Hermes brings me packages, always at night
vanity still plagues him—he is convinced
he will be recognized. Demeter stops by with cuttings
for my garden, we commiserate on the terrible taste
of daughters. Orion teaches archery at my son's summer camp
his millennia in the sky have grounded him.

It surprised me to learn they do not miss their great halls—
they prefer our tiny trusts to pious belief.
The secret of happiness, Hephaestus told me once
before kissing me goodnight,
is good enough.

The Angler

Start at Central Park in Schenectady, NY but feel free
to stop by Rochester on your way to California.
When you make it to the hallway
next to my bedroom at 1 am,
squeeze past my brother crying in his crib,

but don't step on the multiplication flash cards
or my ten-year-old self will not show you
how to open the trick window. Make your way
to Istanbul via Chicago but don't linger too long
or you'll miss your stopover in NYC.
If you get to Poland, you've gone too far.

When you hear the child screaming mid-tantrum,
turn left. Stop in front of the library
next to the boba shop. She is screaming because
you stepped on her shadow
        you zipped up her jacket
                you wiped her nose

you kept her from her full her-ness.

You
she is screaming because of
you.

Lift up the red-faced child,
the child covered in saliva and snot
the child no parent wants to claim,
hold her tightly as she thrashes
like a hooked fish in your embrace
tell her, *I traveled my whole life*
to be here with you.

Your Birthday

How can I tell you that I did not love
you the day you were born.
That my first word to you was why,
my arms strapped down,
my head a balloon thumping against the ceiling.

How can I tell you that I did not love
carrying you. That you hijacked and invaded
every cell, locking doors once inside
a bundle of chaos and pain.

How can I tell you that I did not love
you at night—our world only
the seam of closet light and one confused bird.

How can I tell you that I watched your father
deflate with relief when I finally noticed

my love for you

which, like most lasting love,
grew so slowly, I overlooked it.

When you ask about the day you were born
and I find I must tell you these things, I will also tell you
that love is the salt-speckled used car

that got you through one last winter
every shift a prayer with cables in the backseat
for the battery that won't hold a charge
when you play Russian Roulette with the engine

clutch worn down almost as far as the treads on the tires
you can't afford to replace so you drive an extra mile to avoid
the hill with railroad tracks just in case
but you know life is better with it than without
because love is being grateful for your existence.

Unenlightenment

I unflop myself off the couch
and walk toe-to-heel back up the stairs
where I unkiss my children and unsmooth their blankets.

I unclean them, removing soap,
rubbing dirt onto their skin and into their hair;
I unshout, swallowing volume as they skitter around.

Earlier, I will uneat the raspberry
and place it carefully back on its stem. I will unfeed
the chickens, pulling back the seeds and corn from their greedy beaks.

At the beginning, in bed, I will unsay
what escaped with unlove, and while I am at it, I will unyell,
unask, unembrace, untell. I will un-us, so we can do it all again, but better.

Acknowledgments

I would like to thank the publications where some of these poems first appeared, sometimes in slightly different forms:

Beyond Words "My Neighborhood" and "Your Birthday"

Etched Onyx Magazine "Relationship Inquest," "The Rescue," "Unenlightenment," "You asked me to tell you something obvious"

Evocations Review "Fallen"

Mid-Atlantic Review "Fully Known"

Off Topic Publishing "Abandoned"

Paper Dragon "Book Sale," and "Merry-go-round"

River Heron Review "Do Not Forget to Guard the Calmness"

Rockvale Review "Rage"

Rust & Moth "Ten Dollars"

San Antonio Review "Same Page"

Spoon River Poetry Review "Marionette: Condition Fair" and "Transfigured"

Strix "Switch Off the Nebulas on Your Way Out"

Unleash Lit "Recollection" and "Intersection"

Willows Wept Review "Careless" and "Could we say then, at least, that I am your muse?"

Andi Myles is a Washington DC area science writer by day, poet in the in between times. Her favorite space is the fine line between essay and poetry. Her work has appeared in Rattle, Tahoma Literary Review, and B O D Y, among others.

You can find her at www.andimyles.com.

Also Available from Cathexis Northwest Press:

Something To Cry About
by Robert Krantz

Suburban Hermeneutics
by Ian Cappelli

God's Love Is Very Busy
by David Seung

that one time we were almost people
by Christian Czaniecki

Fever Dream/Take Heart
by Valyntina Grenier

The Book of Night & Waking
by Clif Mason

Dead Birds of New Zealand
by Christian Czaniecki

The Weathering of Igneous Rockforms in High-Altitude Riparian Environments
by John Belk

If A Fish
by George Burns

How to Draw a Blank
by Collin Van Son

En Route
by Jesse Wolfe

sky bright psalms
by Temple Cone

Moonbird
by Henry G. Stanton

southern athiest. oh, honey
by d. e. fulford

Bruises, Birthmarks & Other Calamities
by Nadine Klassen

Wanted: Comedy, Addicts
by AR Dugan

They Curve Like Snakes
by David Alexander McFarland

the catalog of daily fears
by Beth Dufford

Shops Close Too Early
by Josh Feit

Vanity Unfair and Other Poems
by Robert Eugene Rubino

Destructive Heresies
by Milo E. Gorgevska

Bodies of Separation
by Chim Sher Ting

The Night with James Dean and Other Prose Poems
by Allison A. deFreese

About Time
by Julie Benesh

Suspended
by Ellen White Rook

The Unempty Spaces Between
by Louis Efron

Quomodo probatur in conflatorio
by Nick Roberts

Suspended
by Ellen White Rook

Call Me Not Ishmael but the Sea
by J. Martin Daughtry

Wild Evolution
by Naomi Leimsider

Coming To Terms
by Peter Sagnella

Acta
by Patrick Wilcox

Honeymoon Shoes
by Valyntina Grenier

Practising Ascending
by Nadine Hitchiner

Home Visit
by Michal Rubin

LA CIUDAD EN TI: THE CITY WITHIN YOU
by Karla Marrufo
Translated from the Spanish by Allison A. deFreese

Resin in the Milky Way
by Amanda Rabaduex

Bone Hunting
by Trinity Catlin

Muskets for the Bear Problem
by Andrew Whitmer

Self-Portraits as a Reddening Sky
by Samuel Gilpin

Desert
by Eric Larsh

Leaving the Religion of Self-Harm
by Bailey Blumenstock

LA DULZURA DE LOS NAUFRAGIOS: THE SWEETNESS OF SHIPWRECKS
by Karla Marrufo
Translated from the Spanish by Allison A. deFreese

Cathexis Northwest Press

www.ingramcontent.com/pod-product-compliance
Lightning Source LLC
Chambersburg PA
CBHW052125070526
44586CB00016B/2083